The Way of the Cross

Meditations on Encountering Jesus

Tomáš Halík

Paulist Press
New York / Mahwah, NJ

Cover image by KathyDentzKeith/Shutterstock.com
Cover and book design by Lynn Else

Original Title: *Velkopáteční meditace*
© 2020 Tomáš Halík
Translation: © 2021, INSTITUTO MISSIONÁRIO FILHAS DE SÃO PAULO - PAULINAS EDITORA
Rua Francisco Salgado Zenha, 11 - 2685-332 Prior Velho - Portugal
www.paulinas.pt

English translation copyright © 2023 by Paulist Press

Library of Congress Cataloging-in-Publication Data
Names: Halík, Tomáš, author.
Title: The way of the cross : meditations on encountering Jesus / Tomáš Halík.
Other titles: Velkopáteční meditace. English
Description: New York / Mahwah, NJ : Paulist Press, 2023. | "Original Title: Velkopáteční meditace, 2020 Tomáš Halík." | Summary: "Reflections on the Stations of the Cross for personal prayer and reflection"— Provided by publisher.
Identifiers: LCCN 2022029922 (print) | LCCN 2022029923 (ebook) | ISBN 9780809156276 (paperback) | ISBN 9780809187898 (ebook)
Subjects: LCSH: Stations of the Cross—Meditations.
Classification: LCC BX2040 .H2513 2023 (print) | LCC BX2040 (ebook) | DDC 232.96/3—dc23/eng/20221024
LC record available at https://lccn.loc.gov/2022029922
LC ebook record available at https://lccn.loc.gov/2022029923

ISBN 978-0-8091-5627-6 (paperback)
ISBN 978-0-8091-8789-8 (e-book)

Published by Paulist Press
997 Macarthur Boulevard
Mahwah, New Jersey 07430
www.paulistpress.com

Printed and bound in the
United States of America

*In this prayer, I have tried to gather all
the experiences of the church from the period of
persecution under the communist regime.
The Way of the Cross
was an important support in our Christian journey.
Hidden in the woods near Prague,
we recited it, joining the sufferings of Christians
all over the world.
Precisely to them, to the many Christians who
even today are unjustly persecuted,
I would like to dedicate the text of this prayer.*

Invitation to the Journey

Daughters of Jerusalem, do not weep for
me, but weep for yourselves and for your
children. (Luke 23:28)

Let us remember these words of Jesus when, in his footsteps, we begin this Way of the Cross. Jesus and his cross are not something external to our life; they are not an event that ended in the past; they must not be the object of our sentimental piety. Jesus does not invite us on the Way of the Cross to regret him, but to change our mentality and our actions. He wants to take our heart of stone and give us a heart of flesh, truly human, capable of that courage that love requires.

Jesus carried the cross from Pilate's courtyard to Calvary. This road is only part of the whole journey of his life, a life that continues in the history of his church, of humanity, and in the history of each one of us. In our lives and in our history, always and anew, we encounter Jesus who carries the cross.

We often pass by it and often do not recognize it. He comes to meet us as he did with his disciples after his resurrection. It has changed. But he shows us his wounds. We meet him in those who carry the heavy crosses of persecution, of the various types of poverty. We meet him in the wounds of those whom we ourselves have hurt; we also encounter him in our wounds.

With this awareness we now begin this journey in the footsteps of the crucified one, in the places sanctified by the blood of his witnesses, carrying in his heart all the places of our world where his paschal history continues. Let us pray for the healing of our history, our memory, our will, our hearts, and our lives.

I

Last Supper

Just as the bread and wine consumed are no longer perceptible with the human senses, so too the Son of Man would seem to be annulled.

*B*ut just as the bread and wine consumed are not lost but give strength to the body and joy to the human heart, so too the death of Jesus is not a vain descent into nothingness. The life and death of Jesus, in fact, constitute the bread for the human journey.

Jesus dined for the last time with his disciples that night, while the chosen people remembered their exit from the land of slavery to the land of freedom. Jesus also leads humanity toward freedom, and offers himself as food so that we, too, do not stop exhausted and turn back as Israel did.

The freedom that Jesus gives us cannot be given to us by the world. Jesus is the way to freedom, the truth that sets us free and the life that frees us from fear, sin, and death. When together we celebrate the Eucharist, the Lord's Supper, we open ourselves, our lives, our communities, and our whole world to Christ the Liberator.

Let us pray for all the hungry of our world, for all those who are cast out of the tables laid out by the rich and powerful.

Let us pray for those who are hungry and thirsty for justice, truth, love, and human and divine closeness.

Let us pray for the church, that she may become an open and welcoming cenacle for all the hungry.

Let us pray for all the ministers at Christ's table, that they may learn to give of themselves and to carry out his law.

Let us pray that Christ's invitation to be part of the common table of love and fraternity may reach all men. Let us pray for all Christians, that they may bear witness to solidarity with all our other brothers and sisters, because for all Christ carried his cross.

II

The Prayer of Unity

Jesus says goodbye to his disciples. He makes
a new covenant with them that is sealed with
his own blood.

H e gives them a new law, the law of love: "Just as I
have loved you, you also should love one another"
(John 13:34).

The foundation is no longer the law of "whatever
you do to me I will do to you," but it starts from "what
God does for me I do for you!" This commandment is not
easy, because we must always keep learning this gener-
osity of love.

God in Jesus gives us all of himself. God wants us
to act in this way too. In our society, other laws apply;
there are the privileges of power and wealth. "It will

not be so among you," Jesus admonishes his disciples, before sending them on this long journey through history. "Whoever wishes to be first among you must be your slave" (Matt 20:26–28).

Jesus did not come to judge the world, but to save us; he wants the world to believe. He does not ask his disciples to present a mountain of evidence; he asks of us one thing, the mutual love that he has shown us. This love should be an image of divine love, an invitation to fervent love. "No one has greater love than this, to lay down one's life for one's friends" (John 15:13).

Jesus wants the world to believe in his witness to the truth about God's love. This witness is true because he lives a perfect communion with God. The communion of the disciples should be an image of this unity, but they cannot be united among themselves if they are not united to Christ. They must be united with Jesus as he is united to his heavenly Father. We too are called to make this desire for communion the goal of our actions.

Let us pray for the pastors of the church, for the teachers of the faith, that they may truly desire and work with care for this unity.

We ask for the blessing of all those who strive to break down the walls of prejudice, to heal the wounds of the past, to level the trenches where the rusty weapons of past wars have so far remained.

Let us pray for all Christians to become aware that in all of us circulates the same blood of the same body of which each of us is a member.

Let us pray that we may be able to take upon ourselves the cross of Christ as a bridge that overcomes alienation between us and with God.

III

The Darkness of Gethsemane

Leaving the light of the upper room, Jesus goes into the night, toward the darkness of Gethsemane. With him he specifically brings, Peter, James, and John, those who experienced with him the light of Tabor.

In Gethsemane, there is no luminous cloud, one does not hear the voice of God, one does not see Moses with Elijah. There are times in our being with Jesus when we do not wish to be there, when we do not want to build the three tents, when we do not say that it is good for us to be here. If it were up to us, we would like to avoid them or cross them as quickly as possible; so, too, for the apostles, who are so sad and tired that they fall asleep. Jesus awakens us and invites us to be vigilant and to pray.

The hours of darkness and trials are part of the journey of a Christian, of the church, and of history, just as there are moments of joy in which one experiences a superabundant light and the closeness of God. If we have had the grace to live these moments of light, let us keep them fixed in our memory and recall them precisely in the moments in which we live in the dark.

In the personal journey and the dramatic journey of history, we also find the deep valleys of darkness, when we feel the eclipse of God. But God is not dead; he does not sleep. In the dark nights of God's hiddenness, we must live a threefold patience: in faith, in hope, and in love. Love without patience, in fact, is not true love, hope without patience is not true hope, and faith without patience, when one lives the dark hour of trial, is not mature or deep enough. In this way we, too, can be in deep anguish and cry out to remove from us the cup of suffering. Only sincerity in prayer makes our prayer a school in which we learn trust so that we can say "your will be done and not my will."

Let us pray for all those who are experiencing their Gethsemane. For all those who in their lives experience the darkness of the cross, anxiety, and pain.

Let us pray for all those who are depressed, for the sick, for those who are dying, and for people who are losing their loved ones.

Let us pray for all those who find themselves in pain and sadness, that they may receive the gift of prayer and thus be able to experience strength and peace.

Let us pray for those who are called to live patience in love.

Let us pray to be freed from the superficial and immature faith that wants to avoid the cross.

Let us pray for all courageous people who accept and embrace their cross.

IV

The Failure of
the Disciples

The disciples "deserted him and fled."
This is one of the saddest phrases of all the
New Testament.

ooking at the history of the church, looking at its
current state, and looking at our hearts, with sorrow
we can verify that this phrase could often refer to us as
well.

The history of Christianity is not only composed of
the history of the saints, but also of that of so many enemies of Christ and his Gospel. There are times when we,
too, looking at the enemies of the cross of Christ, would

say to them, "This is your time, this is the hour of darkness." We too are sometimes weak, as the first disciples of Christ were, but we are nevertheless called to bring the light of Christ precisely to those moments.

The Gospel reminds us of Peter's presumptuous words, "Even though all become deserters, I will not" (Mark 14:29). Sacred Scripture neither censors nor hides the weaknesses of the apostles; on the contrary, it tells us how quickly and easily Peter betrays his promise of fidelity.

Peter's path is similar to ours: there are ups and downs. After Caesarea's confession, Jesus calls Peter "the rock." Soon after, he will call him Satan. In Peter's words of rejection of the cross, Jesus recognizes the echo of the evil one's threefold temptation, that is, to be a Messiah without the cross. In another page of the Gospel, Peter decides too quickly to walk on the waters behind Jesus. Soon he shifts his gaze to Jesus and begins to think of himself and so he begins to drown in his own fear. Even at this moment, Peter is sinking back into his fear; with cowardice he denies his Lord three times before the rooster crows.

Peter still loses Jesus from his gaze, but it will be Jesus who looks him in the eyes when he is taken to the Sanhedrin. Peter begins to weep: his tears are the baptism for his second conversion.

Let us pray never to drown in our fears, weak-nesses, and sins.

Let us pray that the eyes of our hearts may always be turned to Christ.

Let us pray for the gift of tears, of repentance, for those who turn their backs on the path of the cross of Jesus throughout history.

V

The Judgment at the Sanhedrin

My hour has not yet come, Jesus says to his
mother at the wedding at Cana. When his
hour came, he washed the feet of his disciples
and sat down with them for the Last Supper.

At this hour the Son of God must be glorified by his
Father. But it is also the hour of Jesus's enemies, the
hour of the reign of darkness.

In the darkness of the night, the Sanhedrin gathers.
Here come the experts of the Law and Scripture, those
who must interpret and preserve the Holy Law of God.
They come to judge the living God. The whole journey of

history passes through the benches of judges who feel sure that they know the intentions and the mind of God. They are professionals of religion. They are presumptuous owners of the truth. They understand everything. In their system, there is no room for mystery and surprise.

Yet God has hidden himself before them: he comes before them in the guise of a man captured and accused. He is judged by those who have made the house of God a market, who treat religion as trading with God. Jesus disturbs their affairs and speaks of a kingdom in which their economic laws, their property trades, are not valid. In his kingdom, man possesses only what he has been given. Can such a man be the awaited Messiah, Son of the Most High? "Don't speak to us in pictures, tell us openly."

But they do not accept his answer. They do not even want to listen to it. They have eyes and they do not see; they have ears, but they do not hear. They have transformed the living God into the dead letter of the law. Their heart has now become of stone. They became priests of a dead god.

In the long journey of faith and in history, we always come across new high priests, judges, interpreters of the Law, proud men who are the trustees of the truth, businessmen in the global market of religion, too sure of themselves. They love the first places at the table, the obsequious greetings, the honorary titles, the fine robes with long fringes, and the long entourages; they pray at the street intersections to be seen by all. They are lost in the exterior trappings, and, because of this, their heart is dry and moldy.

"And yet, when the Son of Man comes, will he find faith on earth?" (Matt 18:8). Is it not that he will find a privileged church, powerful religions, full churches, mosques, and synagogues, and chests filled with riches, but empty hearts? What will happen if he finds all this but not faith?

Let us pray that God will protect us from a religion without love, without faith, and without hope.

Let us pray that he may give humility to the pastors of the church and to the teachers of the faith.

Let us pray that he will give us all the gift of spiritual discernment to distinguish between the living God and idols that are mere human projections; to distinguish between living faith and the ideology of a dead past.

Let us pray that we may be able to give precedence not so much to the easy ways of consumerism, but to following of the one who always carries his cross.

VI

The Judgment of Pilate

Throughout history the conflict between truth and power unfolds like a thread. What is truth?

Pilate's question does not express a philosophical thirst for truth, but a contempt for it. Truth—what is it? How much does the truth weigh? What is the truth for? In fact, we experience that power and money decide, those who take this path choose Pilate and deny Jesus.

What kind of kingdom is it that rejects violence? The powerless king is a laughing king. Whoever thinks in this way denies Christ and chooses Barabbas. Yet Pilate, who represents power and violence, proves to be a coward. He is afraid of both his subjects and his superiors. He is afraid of those he despises: both the bosses and the crowd. He fears being defamed in front of the emperor.

Power without truth always stands on feet of clay, even if it has violence at its disposal. Truth is the power of those who have no power. The truth is heard from the mouths of children: the king who does not reign in the truth is naked. We do not fear those who can torture and kill us. You must be afraid of betraying the truth.

What is truth? Jesus does not respond with definitions and theories. He himself is the answer, he himself is the truth. He himself is the power of those who have no power. He himself is the light through which we see the truth of the world and of each one of us.

Let us pray that we will never allow ourselves to be diverted by the light of truth.

Let us pray for those who have power not to use lies and violence.

Let us pray for the church to defend the truth with courage, without bowing before power and violence.

Let us pray for people not to allow themselves to be diverted by demagogy and false messiahs, and to choose Jesus and not Barabbas.

Let us pray to seek and find the truth on the Way of the Cross of Jesus.

VII

Descent into the Hell of Violence

They "pass" Jesus between the religious and civil authorities. From the Sanhedrin, he is taken to Pilate, from there to Herod and then again to Pilate who, finally, delivers him to the cruel hands of the soldiers.

Jesus, in this land, descends into the hell of malice and human violence. For them he is no longer even a man: he is a case, an object, a thing. For how many people, including religious, priests, and theologians, has God ceased to be a mystery and become a case or an object? It has become a theme of contention and demonstrations, the subject of aseptic descriptions, as if it were one thing among others.

How many times has God been brought before the judgment of superb human reason? How many times has his name been abused? How many times has it been written on the insignia of the crusades of power, wealth, and vainglory? How many times have Christians mistaken the living God for an idol that requires human sacrifice?

How many times do we tend to use other sons and daughters of the same Father as objects? How many people are enslaved and commodified? How many are humiliated and exposed to violence? How many are sexually and spiritually abused?

How many hidden crimes against human dignity take place in our families, and also in the church? How often Jesus is mistreated in children, in his younger brothers and sisters? Jesus came to build on earth a civilization of love without limits. In this city of God, the law of love applies as in heaven, so on earth! His enemies build a city on earth where the law of hatred applies as in hell, so also on earth!

Many ideologies, many dictatorial regimes, promised heaven on earth, but in reality, they made the earth a hell. Jesus, already here on earth, descends into the hell of hatred and human cruelty. Where was and where is God in the hell of wars and concentration camps? God is present in those who are persecuted, tortured, mistreated, humiliated, and who suffer violence. "Truly I tell you, just as you did it to one of the least of these who are members of my family, you did it to me" (Matt 25:40).

Let us pray for those who suffer violence.

Let us pray for the church, so that in countries under a dictatorial regime she may have the strength to stand on the side of freedom and justice.

Let us pray for those who call themselves Christians to bring Christ's peace, reconciliation, and forgiveness into a world full of conflict and violence.

Let us pray for our mother earth, exposed to the violence of exploitation. Let us pray that the cross of Christ will give all the weak strength and hope.

VIII

Women on the Way of the Cross

Women played an important role in the life of Jesus.

Mary, who wanted to be his disciple, was defended by the Lord from her sister's criticism. In the circle of his faithful, both the male and female disciples have had their place. Mary Magdalene was made the first witness of the resurrection, "apostle to the apostles."

We also meet women on the Way of the Cross. Amid the crowd of the curious or indifferent, pressing on the sides of the path, Veronica appears. Jesus imprints the seal of his face on the veil of compassion offered to him by this simple woman. Then there are also the professionals of mourning, whom Jesus reproaches by saying "do not weep for me, but weep for yourselves and for your children" (Luke 23:28).

With these words, however, Jesus also reproaches us and invites us to avoid a false sentimentality in our journey of personal piety. The Way of the Cross is also the path of our conversion. Let us look at Jesus, and at the same time let us look with humility into our hearts.

The women were also present at the foot of the cross of Jesus. When the disciples fled, hid, and disowned him, the women persevered in the dark hour of his death; "the strong woman, that would stand by him." The Way of the Cross of Jesus continues throughout history. Many women have carried and continue to carry his cross with courage. Their value "surpasses pearls and gold" (cf. Job 28:18–19).

Let us pray for the abused and humiliated women, let us pray for all the mothers who are grieved because of the many war camps that still exist in the world today.

Let us pray for sisters who show compassion and mercy.

Let us pray for the recognition of the dignity of women in society and in the church.

Let us pray for the ability to stand firm under the cross, to be able to accompany those who are unjustly accused and persecuted.

IX

Jesus Is Counted among the Evildoers

Jesus begins his public life by putting himself
in the ranks of the sinners who ask John for
the baptism of penance. Jesus ends his life on
this crucified earth between the two thieves:
"He was counted among the evildoers" (see
Luke 22:37).

He, the only one without sin, lines up with us sinners.
He does not stand on the other side to point to the
sinner with a finger. When he raises his voice to those
who want to throw stones at sinners, the stones fall from
their hands, clenched in their fists.

Jesus offers his table to sinners, eats with them. It provokes the wrath of those who think they are righteous. He came for the sick, not for the healthy; he came for sinners, not for the righteous. He opens the eyes of the blind and exposes the blindness of those who think they see, know, and are wise and holy.

The thief on the right recognizes his guilt and trusts in the coming of God's kingdom of mercy. Jesus opens the door of paradise to him.

Let us pray that the Lord will preserve us from pride and presumption.

Let us pray that the Lord will forgive our contempt for others.

Let us pray for the courage to confess our sins, so that the Lord may remember us when he comes to "lower the powerful from their thrones and raise up the humble, to fill the hungry with goods and to send the rich back empty-handed."

Let us pray that, with the power of his cross, Jesus may also open the gates of paradise to us and to all sinners.

X

The Hell of Abandonment

On the cross, Jesus's feet and hands were pierced: "Father, forgive them; for they do not know what they are doing" (Luke 23:34).

From the cross, however, another cry can also be heard: "My God, my God, why have you forsaken me?" (Matt 27:46). This cry is as if it rose from the deepest wound, the one in the heart of Jesus.

In the darkness of suffering and death, Jesus descends into the underworld. He descends into the hell of human cruelty, and then also into the hell of the deepest abandonment: he feels abandoned by his heavenly

Father. In reference to Jesus, Saint Paul writes these scandalous words: "For our sake he made him to be sin who knew no sin" (2 Cor 5:21). Sin, in fact, is separation, alienation from God. Jesus wears the cross of this infernal solitude.

Jesus's cry, however, is not one of despair. Jesus, in the solitude of his pain, asks what all this is for, what meaning it has. He transforms his pain into a question, addressed to his heavenly Father. His question becomes a prayer. Even in our hearts in times of pain, difficult questions arise. Let us turn these questions into prayer. God does not let his Son's question remain unanswered: his answer is the light of Easter morning. God raises his Son from the underworld of loneliness and the darkness of death. "God also highly exalted him and gave him the name that is above every name, so that at the name of Jesus every knee should bend, in heaven and on earth and under the earth" (Phil 2:911).

Let us pray for all those who suffer the hell of human cruelty, the flames of war and violence.

Let us pray for those who feel forgotten and abandoned by God.

Let us pray for those who do not know God.

Let us pray to the one who with his cross conquered fear, sin, and death.

XI

Mary under the Cross

Jesus hangs on the cross, between heaven
and earth. He was deprived of his place on
earth, of his friends, of his clothing, of all
forms of human honor.

He delivered everything and as a last gift, he also
delivers his mother. "'Woman, here is your son.'
Then he said to the disciple, 'Here is your mother'" (John
19:26–27). To the disciple he loved—a symbol of the
great family of the church—Jesus gives his mother and,
together with the Apostle John, we too are entrusted to
her maternal care.

The word of the prophet Simeon has been ful-
filled. Jesus reveals the mystery of so many hearts; he

has become a sign of contradiction. Mary's heart was pierced by the sword of pain.

Hail mother, full of divine light, blessed are you among women. Hail morning star, in the long nights of suffering! Hail Mother of Hope, in the hours of mortal anguish. Hail Queen of the poor and the wretched. Consolation of the afflicted, help for the sick, refuge for sinners. Blessed are you who untie the knots on the rope of our life. Blessed are you, the champion of faith, who confidently accepted the word of God.

At the beginning of creation there is a great divine *fiat*: *fiat lux*, Let there be light! Let there be heaven and earth! Let there be man and woman! At the beginning of the redemption is Mary's fiat: *Fiat mihi secundum voluntas tua* ("Let it be with me according to your word" [Luke 1:38]). This yes of Mary is the door through which God enters in a new way into the world and into history.

Let us pray for mothers who are in pain.

Let us pray for women who have the courage to become mothers, bringing new hope to the world.

Let us pray for the maternal face of our church.

Let us pray to be able to persevere like Mary under the shadow of the cross.

XII

The Delivery of the Spirit

Jesus completed his work on earth. Into the hands of the Father, he delivers his Spirit.

To us he gave himself, his body, his blood, his life, and his death, and, finally, he will also give his Spirit. Jesus will pass through the closed doors of our fears. He will breathe on his disciples, as the creator did with Adam by giving him the breath of life. Adam rises from the dust of nothingness and becomes a living being, an image of the creator. The faith of the disciples in the hour of trial was annulled and became like dust again: "They return to their dust...then you give back the Spirit and they will be recreated" (see Ps 104:29–30).

As in the vision of the prophet Ezekiel, the valley of withered bones, with the power of the divine Spirit, will turn into a host of God's servants.

There are times when, even today, Jesus's disciples are closed in their fear. There are times when even the church resembles a valley of dry bones. God, however, again restores his Spirit, sends his prophets to resurrect faith and hope. It shows that love is stronger than death.

His Spirit comes in the thunder of Pentecost and in the silent and almost imperceptible murmur of the light breeze. One of the expressions of the Spirit is the ability to allow understanding in the diversity of cultures and in the distances of peoples.

Even today, from the ruins of the many towers of Babel arise conflicts, inability, disinterest in coming together. The Spirit of Jesus, however, overcomes and destroys the walls that we build between us. It wants to unify families, cities, nations, churches, and divided religions. Everything wants to unify in Christ.

We believe that at the end of the story, an embrace of Jesus awaits us, an embrace that is always open. On the way to this Omega point we need infinite patience; we need a holy restlessness of the heart, the same of which Saint Augustine spoke.

On the way to the final goal of history, we must not stop at one point, we must not be satisfied with a given situation of the world and of the church. We are a community of pilgrims; on our journey we see divine things only as in a mirror.

Let us pray that God will give us an open heart for the gift of his Spirit.

Let us pray that he may lift his faithful from the dust of nothingness and renew them with his Spirit.

Let us pray that with the preaching of the prophets and with the strength of his Spirit, he may awaken and heal his church, bring it to life and reunite it.

Let us pray that God may give us the patience of hope and the impatience of love.

From the Embrace
of the Mother to the
Embrace of the Earth

Through Mary's joy and into her welcoming
arms, Jesus entered this world; now the
world, through Mary, brings him back into the
same arms, welcoming him in sorrow. Finally,
the dead Jesus is carried by Mary's arms to
the embrace of mother earth.

The one who first came to visit Jesus in the night is no
longer afraid to be recognized. Nicodemus, together
with Joseph of Arimathea, lay the body of Jesus in a

tomb. The stone is rolled and the guards are placed. This is how this story had to end. In the calculations of the powerful, history was not to go beyond Good Friday.

But love is stronger than death. There is no stone large and heavy enough to stop love.

Easter morning brings God's answer to Jesus's question, as well as to ours, about the meaning of the cross, suffering, and death. Suffering and death are part of human history, but they are not the last words. Death is not God, and it can never have absolute power over us.

God is love and is stronger than death. Whoever continually dies in love to himself and to his own selfishness, remains alive forever in God. Such a man becomes a seed that bears so much fruit. It becomes wheat for the bread of life.

$$\smile$$

Let us pray for those who have gone before us, that God's embrace may become the final goal of their journey.

Let us pray for those who, in the dark valleys of pain, struggle for faith and hope, that they may experience the love that endures everything and never ends.

Let us pray for our mother earth, who welcomed and germinated Christ: "Open the heavens and rain from above! Open yourself, O earth, and you will be the savior!"

XIV

The Transfigured Wounds

Jesus returns changed by the experience of
death. Even the people closest and dearest to
him cannot recognize him.

H e approaches the disciples on the road to Emmaus
as an unknown stranger. It also happens to us that
Jesus approaches us as a stranger, and we are not able to
recognize and welcome him. He accompanies us on our
roads and on our journeys and teaches us, in a new way,
how to understand the great story of the Bible. When we
are caught up in fear of the world around us, He passes
through the closed doors of our fears. When we don't

recognize him, he shows us his wounds. When Pilate handed Jesus over for the scourging, he pointed to his wounds by declaring, "Behold the man!" (see John 19:5).

When the apostle Thomas sees his wounds, he exclaims, "My Lord and my God" (John 20:28). Pilate sees in Jesus's wounds his defeated humanity. Thomas, on the other hand, sees his divinity shining. Jesus also comes to us and shows us his wounds. The path of Jesus's cross is not finished. Throughout history there are people wounded both in body and soul. In their suffering the passion of Jesus continues. Jesus stands in solidarity with all the wounded. Only one who does not close his eyes to the wounds of our world can exclaim, "My Lord and my God."

Let us pray for those who have been wounded by the church and in the church.

Let us pray that the church will become a field hospital, so that she will not be the one who hurts, but the one who takes care of the wounds.

Let us pray that the world may experience the healing power of faith.

In the history of the world, the Way of the Cross continues; the mystery of Christ's resurrection also continues. The resurrection takes place where people experience Christ as living. Why do we seek the one who is alive among the dead? Why do we seek in the past the one who is the absolute future of the world and of each one of us?

> Christ yesterday and today
> the Beginning and the End
> the Alpha
> and the Omega
> All time belongs to him
> and all the ages
> To him be glory and power
> Through every age and forever. Amen.
> By his holy
> and glorious wounds,
> may Christ the Lord
> guard us
> and protect us. Amen.

> (*The Roman Missal – Preparation of
> the Paschal Candle, Easter Vigil*)